My First Book
of
Bible Promises

Carine Mackenzie

CF4•K

© Copyright 2005 Carine Mackenzie
ISBN: 978-1-84550-039-9
Reprinted 2009

Published by
Christian Focus Publications, Geanies House, Fearn,
Ross-shire, IV20 1TW, Great Britain.

www.christianfocus.com
email:info@christianfocus.com
Cover design by Alister MacInnes
Cover illustrations by Diane Mathes
Publication illustrations by Diane Mathes

Scripture based on the New King James Version.
Copyright © 1982 by Thomas Nelson, Inc.
Used by permission. All rights reserved.

Printed and bound by
Bell and Bain, Glasgow

Mixed Sources
Product group from well-managed
forests and other controlled sources
www.fsc.org Cert no. TT-COC-002769
© 1996 Forest Stewardship Council
FSC

From the Author

God's word is faithful and true. He has made many promises to his people, which we are to believe.

The promises will encourage us when we are afraid, or troubled by sin.

His promises help us to pray and guide us through life.

They remind us of his care and love to us, of his many blessings and the promise of salvation through Jesus Christ.

All of us have to face death, and eternity beyond that. Our sin deserves God's anger and punishment, but Jesus suffered and died on the cross to pay the price for the sins of his people. Jesus Christ has promised to save all who believe in him.

Carine Mackenzie

Contents

God Cares

1 Kings 8:56
There has not failed one word of all God's good promise.

Hebrews 10:23
He who promises is faithful.

In the Bible we read many promises that God has given to his people. God never breaks a promise. He never forgets what he has promised. God's promises are always reliable.

Genesis 8:22
While the earth remains, seedtime and harvest, cold and heat, winter and summer, and day and night shall not cease.

God has promised the order of the seasons every year. He has promised the day and the night in each 24 hour period. God is in control of the whole universe.

Genesis 9:13,15

I set my rainbow in the cloud and it shall be for the sign of the covenant between me and the earth: ... the waters shall never again become a flood to destroy all flesh.

The rainbow is a reminder of God's promise that he will never destroy the world again by water. He has promised that one day he will destroy this world with fire.
(See 2 Peter 3:10)

Hebrews 13:5
God himself has said, 'I will never leave you nor forsake you.'

What a comfort to know that God is always with us. Our dearest family member or closest friend will have to leave us one day, but God will always be with his children.

Genesis 28:15
I am with you and will keep you wherever you go.

God spoke this promise first to Jacob but it is true for all who believe in him. Wherever you go, God will keep you.

Philippians 4:19

My God will supply all your need according to his riches in glory by Christ Jesus.

All that we have comes from God. His provision for us of food, clothing, friends, family and lots more shows his wonderful love and blessing.

Psalm 121:3-4

He who keeps you will not slumber. He, who keeps Israel, shall neither slumber nor sleep.

God is always watching over us. We can rest and sleep in peace because God is our guard.

God Blesses

Proverbs 8:17

I love those who love me, and those who seek me early will find me.

It is wise to seek the
Lord Jesus early in life.
God has promised that
those who seek
him diligently will
find him.
It is never too
soon to seek the
Lord Jesus.

Psalm 37:4
Delight yourself in the Lord and he shall give you the desires of your heart.

If we love God and love to think about him, then the desire of our heart will be to know him more.
God has promised this.
True satisfaction is found in God alone.

Psalm 29:11
The Lord will give strength to his people; the Lord will bless his people with peace.

The strong and mighty Lord Jesus promises strength to his people when they feel weak; and peace when they feel troubled or anxious.

Matthew 6:33

Seek first the kingdom of God and his righteousness, and all these things shall be added to you.

The most important thing in life is to be right with God, to be trusting in the Lord Jesus alone for salvation. God knows what we need, and he will take care of us.

Deuteronomy 15:18

The Lord your God will bless you in all that you do.

This promise was given
to those who were
generous and fair
to others. The
Lord has promised
special care and
love to them.
The blessing of
God is the best gift
we can receive.

Psalm 23:6
Surely goodness and mercy shall follow me all the days of my life.

God's goodness supplies all our needs. God's mercy blots out our sin. This happens because Jesus suffered and died for us on the cross. These wonderful blessings are promised to God's people all their life.

God Guides

Proverbs 3:5-6

Trust in the Lord with all your heart, and lean not on your own understanding. In all your ways acknowledge him and he shall direct your paths.

God will guide us if we trust him and pray to him for help. We should use his word to show us the right way to live.

Psalm 48:14

For this is God, our God, forever and ever. He will be our guide even to death.

We need a guide all through life, when we are young and when we are old. God is the same today and always.
With God and his word as our guide, we will be safe in this life and forever.

John 16:13

When the Spirit of truth has come, he will guide you into all truth.

God the Holy Spirit has promised to guide us as we read God's word and think about it. God's word is truth and we will not understand it properly without his help and guidance.

Exodus 33:14

My presence will go with you, and I will give you rest.

God does not just give instructions to guide us. He actually comes with us to guide us as we go. If he is with us, we will have rest.

God's Word

Mark 13:31
Heaven and earth will pass away, but my words will never pass away.

God's word is inspired and enduring. The world will come to an end one day. God promises that his word will last forever.

Isaiah 55:11

My word ... shall not return to me empty, but it shall accomplish what I please, and it shall prosper in the thing for which I sent it.

God's word works. He has promised that it will always do what he intends it to do. God uses his word to bring people to himself and to help them to grow in grace and in knowledge of Jesus Christ.

1 Peter:24-25,
Isaiah 40:8

The grass withers and its flower falls away, but the word of the Lord endures forever.

All human beings and human
wisdom will pass away like
withering flowers.
God's word will
never pass away.
It is unchanging,
always true.

John 5:24

He who hears my word and believes in him who sent me, has everlasting life and shall not come into judgment. But has passed from death unto life.

When we hear God's word to us in the Bible, we must believe it and trust in God who sent Jesus to die for us. The promise of God is then everlasting life. We will not be punished for our sins because Christ has paid the price.

God's
Salvation

John 6:37
All that the Father gives me will come to me, and the one who comes to me I will never cast out.

No one who comes to
Christ will be cast
away. With all our
faults and sins and
weakness, Jesus
will not refuse.
Those who come
to him, have been
given to him by the
Father.

John 3:16

For God so loved the world that he gave his one and only Son that whoever believes in him should not perish but have everlasting life.

God's love is so big we cannot measure it.
He gave the most wonderful
gift Jesus Christ, his Son.
God promised that if we
believe in his Son we will
not perish but will have
eternal life.

Romans 6:23

The wages of sin is death, but the gift of God is eternal life in Christ Jesus our Lord.

Our sin deserves the punishment of death, but through Jesus Christ, God has promised the free gift of eternal life to those who believe and trust him.

Acts 16:31

Believe on the Lord Jesus Christ and you will be saved, you and your household.

This was the gospel message for the Philippian jailer. He was told to trust the Lord Jesus as his Saviour for himself. The good news of the gospel was also for his whole family. If they believed in the Lord Jesus Christ, they too would be saved.

Eternity

1 John 2:25

And this is the promise that he has promised us — eternal life.

When our bodies die — that is not the end of life. The souls of believers are made perfect and immediately pass into heaven. Our bodies rest in the grave until they are raised again at the last day. God promises his people life that shall never end. Those who are not God's people, will suffer in hell — an awful place prepared for the devil and his angels.

John 14:19
Because I live, you will live also.

We have the promise and the hope of eternal life, because Jesus rose again from the dead and is alive now.

John 13:1

Having loved his own which were in the world, he loved them unto the end.

God's love reaches everywhere. It is perfect and full. He loves his own all through their lives, right to death and beyond.

John 14:3

And if I go and prepare a place for you, I will come again and receive you to myself, that where I am there you may be also.

Jesus went to the cross at Calvary to prepare a place in heaven for each one of his people. He will come to the earth once more to take his people to heaven with himself.

Psalm 73:24
You will guide me with your counsel and afterwards receive me to glory.

God's wise counsel guides us through life. At the end of life, we don't need to be frightened. God has promised to receive us in heaven and welcome us to glory.

John 10:28
I give them eternal life, and they shall never perish, neither shall anyone snatch them out of my hand.

Those who love Jesus are completely safe with him. Nothing can snatch them away from his care. Jesus has all power to keep them secure.

Prayer

Micah 7:7

My God will hear me.

If we can truly say that God is 'my God' then we can confidently say that he will hear us. He has promised to listen to those whom he loves.

Matthew 6:6

When you pray, go into your room, and when you have shut your door, pray to your Father in secret; and your Father who sees in secret will reward you openly.

It is good to pray in private without boasting about it to others God hears our secret prayers and has promised to answer them openly.

Matthew 7:7

Ask and it will be given you, seek and you will find; knock and it will be opened to you.

God has the answer for everything. It is a great privilege to ask him for our needs, to seek his love and to knock for access to his presence.

John 14:14
If you ask anything in my name, I will do it.

To pray in the name of Jesus, is to pray in a way that pleases and honours him. It is not a selfish prayer but it is a prayer for the glory of Jesus, and for his kingdom. It is not just adding 'for Jesus' sake' at the end of our prayer.

Isaiah 65:24
Before they call, I will answer; and while they are still speaking, I will hear.

God knows us better than we know ourselves. Sometimes the answer to our prayer is on the way, before we even pray. God provides for every need.

James 1:5

If any of you lack wisdom, let him ask of God, who gives to all liberally and without reproach, and it will be given to him.

We all lack wisdom and need God's help for every day. God has promised the necessary wisdom to those who ask him in faith.

Sin

James 4:7-8

Submit to God, resist the devil and the devil will flee from you. Draw near to God and God will draw near to you.

If God is our Lord, the devil is defeated. If we resist the devil, he will be forced away, and God will be very near to us.

1 John 1:9

If we confess our sins, he is faithful and just to forgive us our sins, and to cleanse us from all unrighteousness.

Sin leaves a stain on our lives.
If we confess our sins to our faithful and just Father God, he will deal with that stain. He will forgive every sin through Jesus Christ.

Psalm 103:8,10

The Lord is merciful and gracious... He has not dealt with us according to our sins, nor punished us according to our iniquities.

Our sins deserve great punishment. God has graciously accepted the suffering of 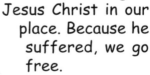 Jesus Christ in our place. Because he suffered, we go free.

Matthew 1:21
You shall call his name JESUS, for he will save his people from their sins.

When God the Son came to this world as a baby, Joseph was told by God the Father to give him the name JESUS, which means 'Saviour'. The promise was given that he would save his people from their sins. This is what Jesus has done by dying on the cross and taking the punishment of our sins.

47

Proverbs 28:13

He who covers his sins will not prosper, but whoever confesses and forsakes them will have mercy.

If we try to cover up our sin and pretend we have done nothing wrong, we will be in big trouble. But if we tell God about our sin and turn away from it, God promises to have mercy and forgive.

Jeremiah 31:34
Hebrews 10:17

I will forgive their iniquity and their sin
I will remember no more.

God promises not only to forgive the
sin of his people,
but to forget it
completely.
Our sins are
blotted out by the
blood of Jesus Christ
who died on the cross at
Calvary. We should trust
him and love him, who
first loved us.

Fear

Matthew 11:28

Come to me, all you who labour and are heavy laden, and I will give you rest.

If we come to Jesus with our problems of sadness, loneliness and anxiety, he has promised to help us and give us peace in our hearts.

Isaiah 41:10
Fear not, for I am with you; be not dismayed, for I am your God. I will strengthen you, yes, I will help you, I will uphold you with my righteous right hand.

God often tells us not to be afraid. He has promised to be with us, to strengthen, help and uphold.
With these wonderful promises from the faithful God, we should never be afraid.

Philippians 4:6-7

Be anxious for nothing, but in everything by prayer and supplication, with thanksgiving, let your requests be made to God; and the peace of God which surpasses all understanding will guard your hearts and minds through Christ Jesus.

God asks us to pray thankfully to him about everything. He then gives us 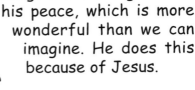 his peace, which is more wonderful than we can imagine. He does this because of Jesus.

Psalm 34:19

Many are the afflictions of the righteous, but the Lord delivers him out of them all.

God does not promise an easy life with no problems. He tells us we will have difficulties. But he will be with us and take us through all our problems.

2 Corinthians 12:9

My grace is sufficient for you, for my strength is made perfect in weakness.

When we are weak, God's strength is shown more clearly. He gives us the grace that we need, just when we need it.

Psalm 55:22

Cast your burden on the Lord and he shall sustain you.

God asks us to tell him all our problems. He wants to carry them for us. If we trust him, he will uphold us in all the struggles of life.

Deuteronomy 31:8

The Lord is the one who goes before you. He will be with you; he will not leave you nor forsake you; do not fear nor be dismayed.

God is with us everywhere. If we travel far away, go to live in a new town, start in a new school — he is there too. His promise never fails.

Memory record

Tick each book once you have learned each promise.

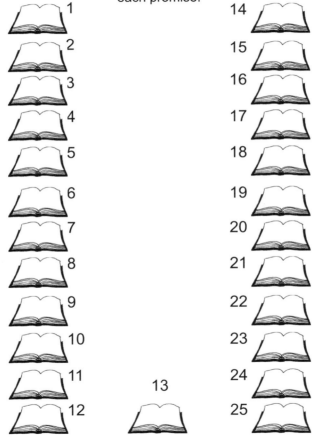

Memory record

Tick each book once you have learned each promise.

26		39
27		40
28		41
29		42
30		43
31		44
32		45
33		46
34		47
35		48
36	38	49
37		50

Look out for

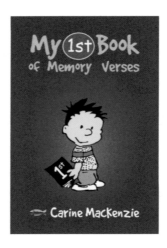

The truth that we learn as children can be brought back to our memory at vital stages in later life. Scripture memorising will prove to be a priceless treasure to our children for today and for all of their lives.

ISBN: 978-1-85792-783-2

Look out for

114 profound Questions and Answers. If you have ever wanted to know how to explain the Christian faith to young children in bite-sized chunks, then 'My 1st Book of Questions & Answers' will be of great help to you. An invaluable tool to get you started.

ISBN: 978-1-85792-570-8

Look out for

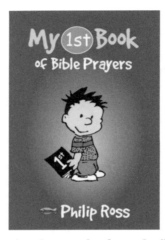

Children need to be taught from God's word. We all need to learn from him in order to become wise. Scripture memorisation, prayer and worship should be part of your daily routine. The disciples asked the Lord Jesus to teach them to pray. Ask God to teach you and your children to do the same.

ISBN 978-1-85792-944-7